Piano • Vocal • Guitar

CLAPTON

T0056003

ISBN 978-1-61774-293-4

HAL•LEONARD® CORPORATION

7777 W. BLUEMOUND RD. P.O. BOX 13819 MILWAUKEE, WI 53213

CONTENTS

4   Travelin' Alone

11   Rocking Chair

16   River Runs Deep

24   Judgement Day

28   How Deep Is the Ocean

34   My Very Good Friend, the Milkman

38   Can't Hold Out Much Longer

42   That's No Way to Get Along

48   Everything Will Be Alright

55   Diamonds Made from Rain

61   When Somebody Thinks You're Wonderful

65   Hard Times Blues

70   Run Back to Your Side

77   Autumn Leaves

TRAVELIN' ALONE

Words and Music by
MELVIN "LIL' SON" JACKSON

I ain't gon'

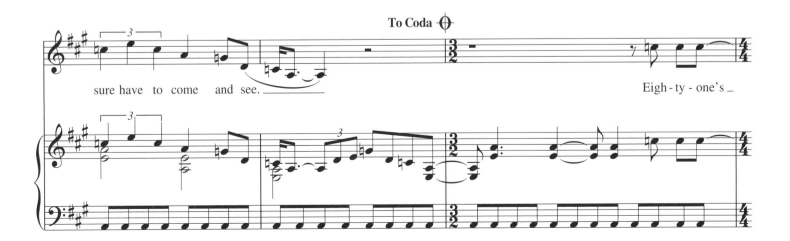

in the yard and two's out on the road.

Eigh-ty-one's in the yard and two's out on the road.

Eigh-ty-one makes her liv-in', eigh-ty-

two'll put you out of door. No-bod-y knows

I'm trou - bled but the dear Lord a - bove.

No - bod-y knows I'm trou - bled but the dear Lord a - bove.

Well you know how I feel, you

ev - er have been in love.

Lord, I

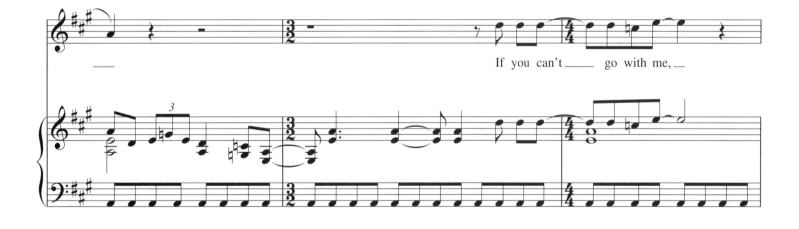

CODA

A7

ROCKIN' CHAIR

Words and Music by
HOAGY CARMICHAEL

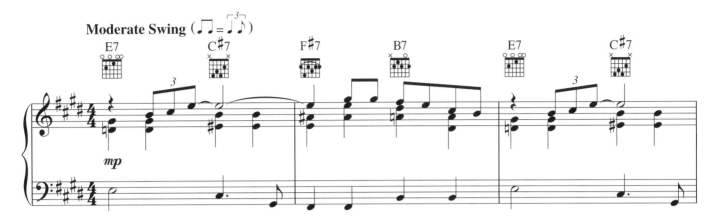

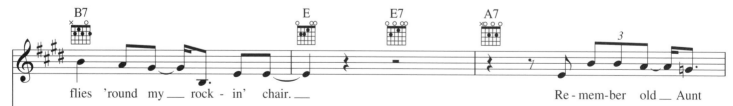

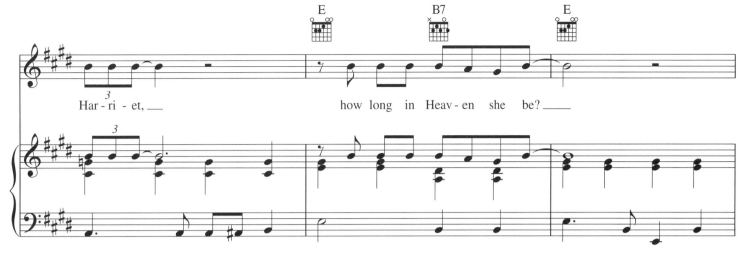

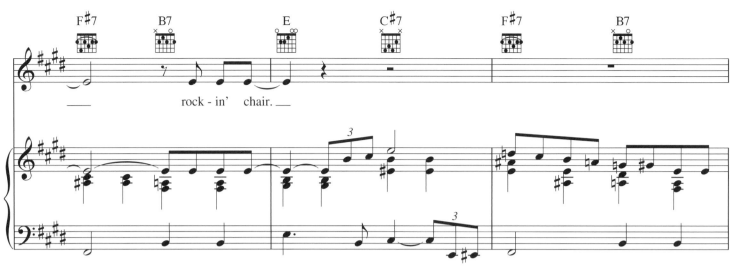

rock - in' chair. ___

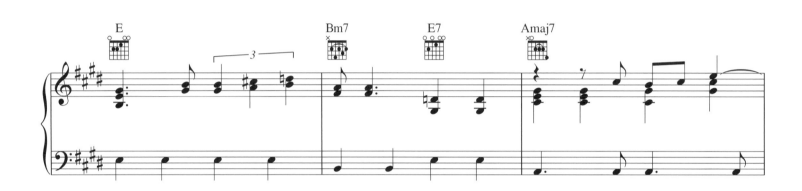

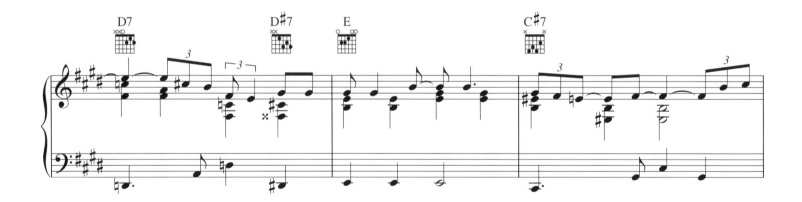

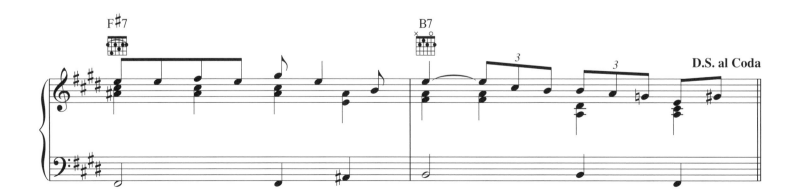

D.S. al Coda

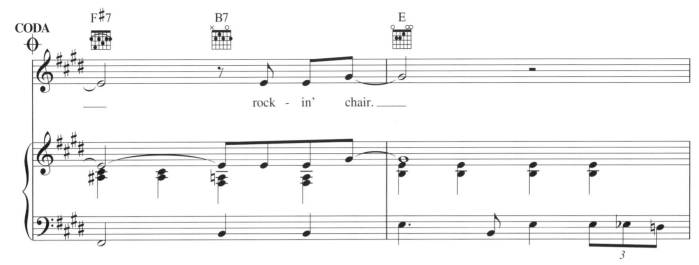

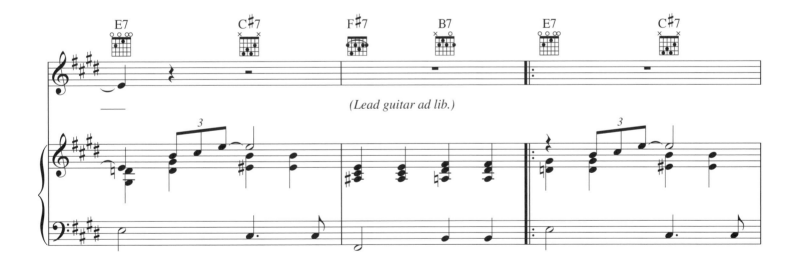

RIVER RUNS DEEP

Words and Music by
JOHN CALE

Moderately

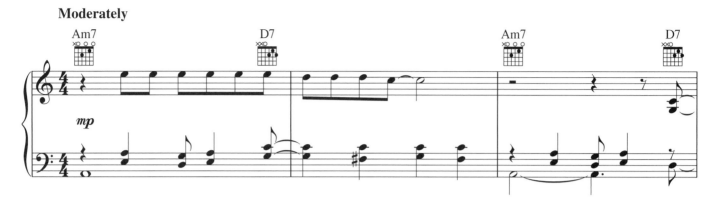

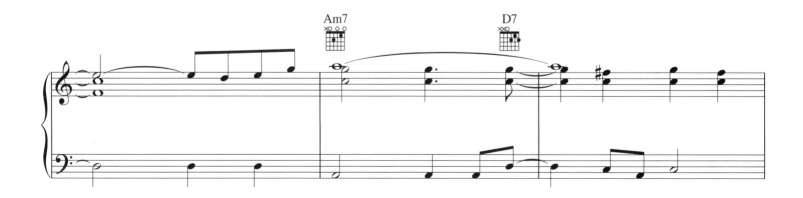

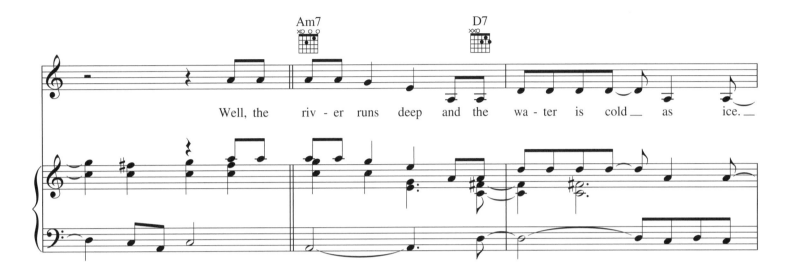

Well, the riv - er runs deep and the wa - ter is cold __ as __ ice. __

The riv - er runs deep and the

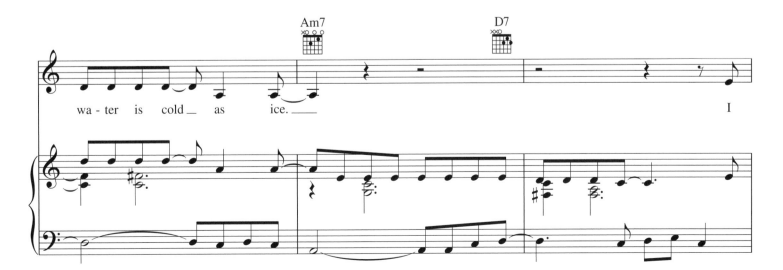

wa - ter is cold __ as __ ice. ____

I

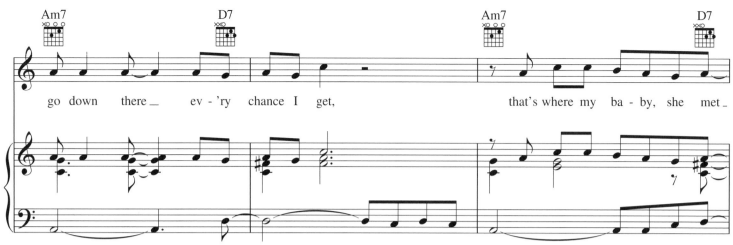

go down there __ ev - 'ry chance I get, that's where my ba - by, she met __

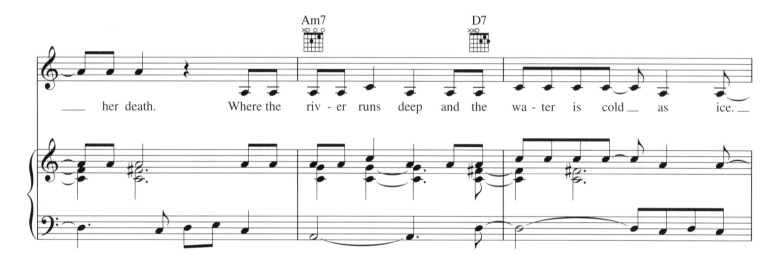

__ her death. Where the riv - er runs deep and the wa - ter is cold __ as ice. __

Ain't no wom - an gon - na

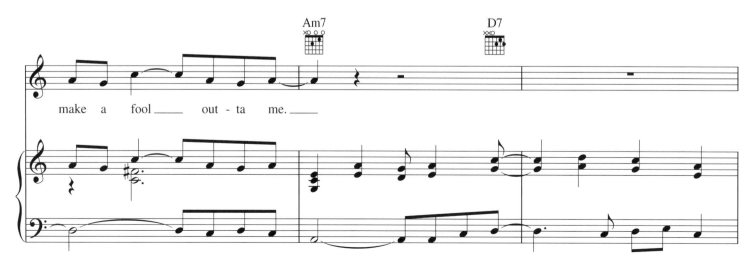

make a fool __ out - ta me. __

Ain't no wom-an gon-na make a fool___ out-ta me.___

Run - nin' 'round, that's ___ what they said.

She's at the bot-tom of the riv - er bed. Well, the riv - er runs deep, the

wa - ter is cold ___ as ice. ___

(Ad lib instrumental solo.)

Play 8 times

Cheat - in' wom - an gon - na

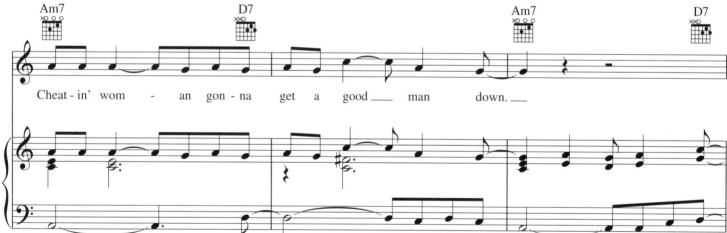

get a good man down. ___

Cheat - in' wom - an gon - na get a good ___ man down. ___

Run - nin' 'round like a sil - ly fool,

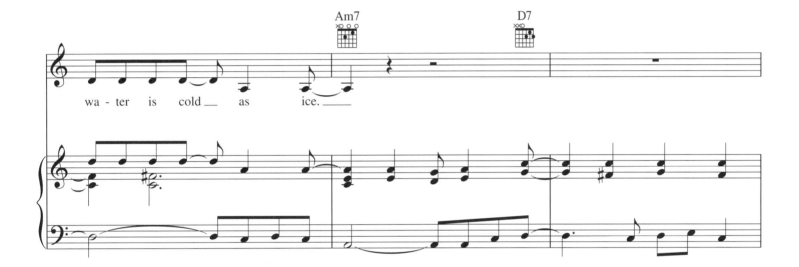

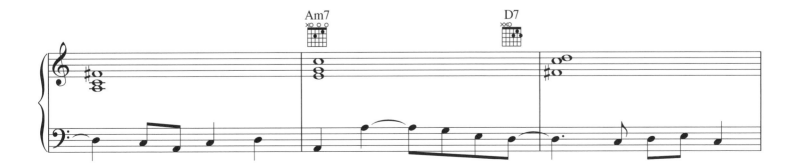

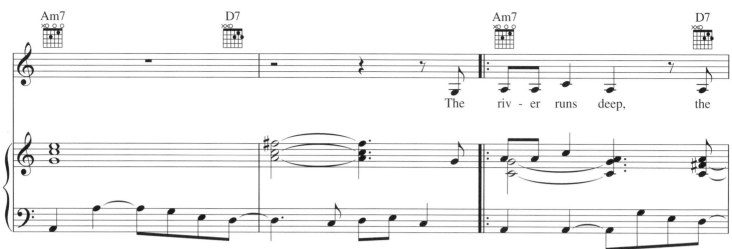

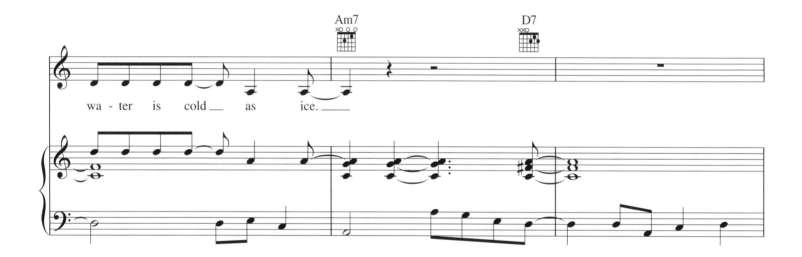

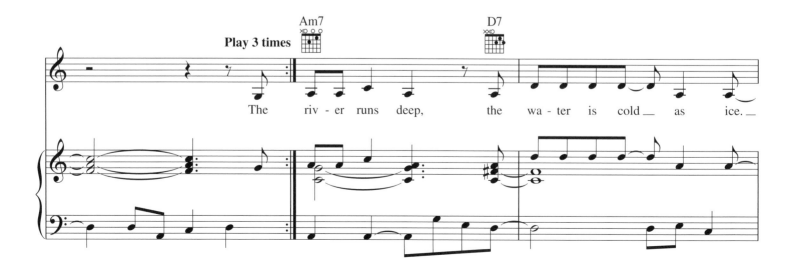

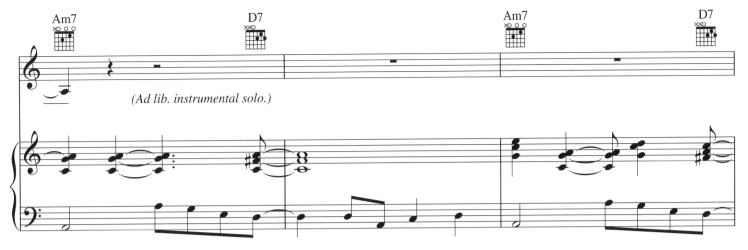

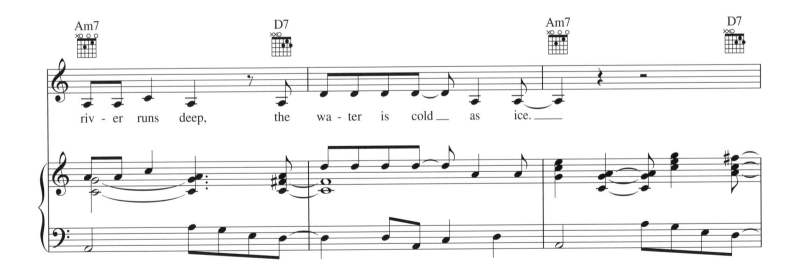

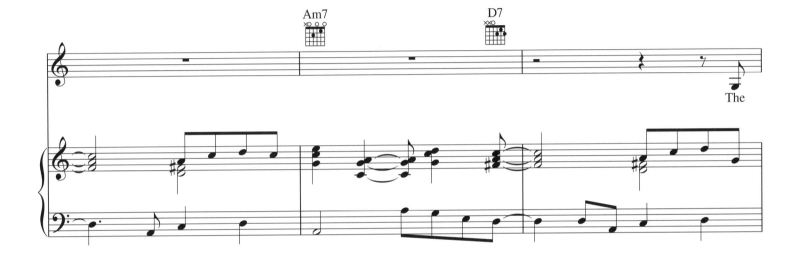

JUDGEMENT DAY

Words and Music by
JAMES PRYOR

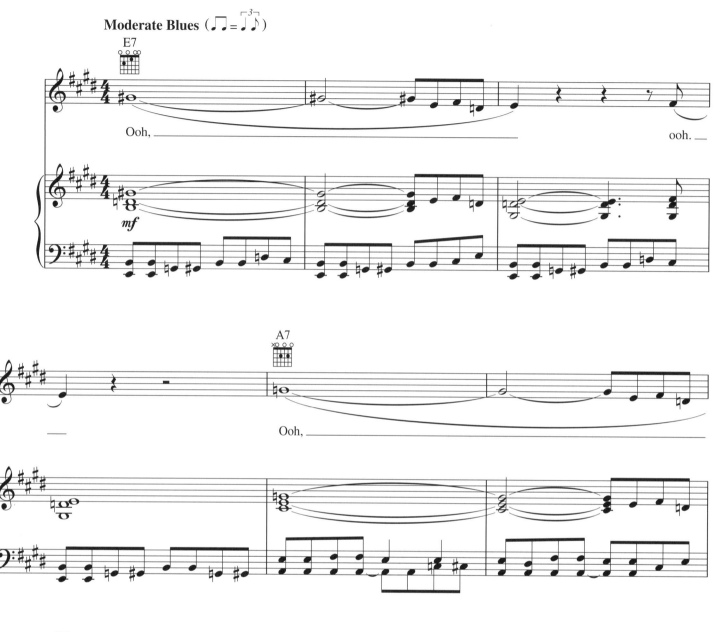

Tell- in' Saint Pet - er, "Won't you o - pen the door?"
Tell __ my friends __ that I gone __ to rest. __
You gon - na cry ___ your ___ blues ___ a - way.

Yes, I'm com - in'.

(Yes, I'm com - in'.) Yes, I'm com - in'. (Yes, I'm com - in'.)

Yes, I'm com - in' ___ just like __ my time ain't long.

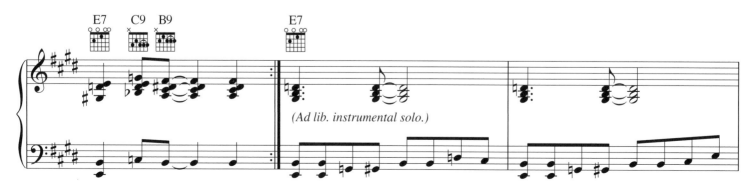

(Ad lib. instrumental solo.)

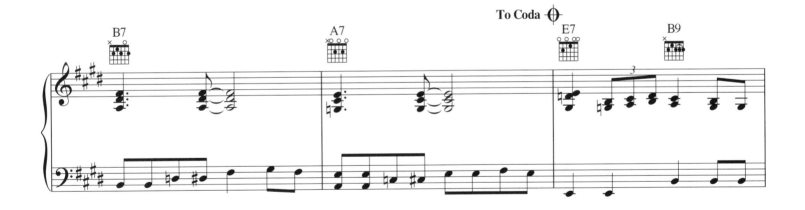

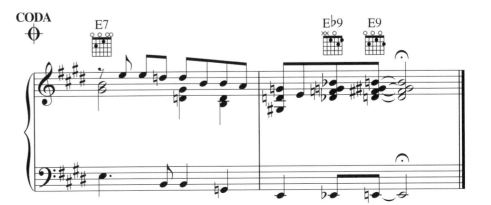

HOW DEEP IS THE OCEAN
(How High is the Sky)

Words and Music by
IRVING BERLIN

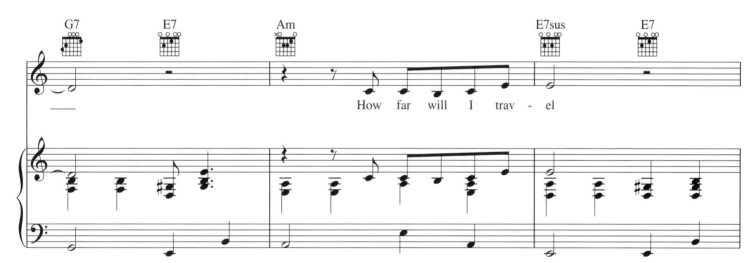

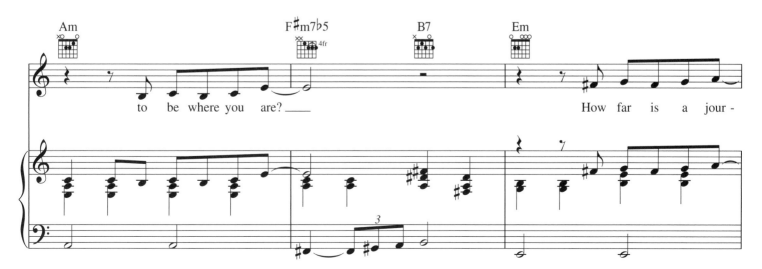

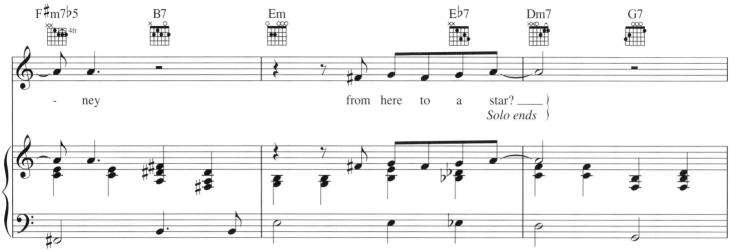

- ney   from here to a star? _____
Solo ends

And __ if I ev - er lose you, __   how much would I cry? __

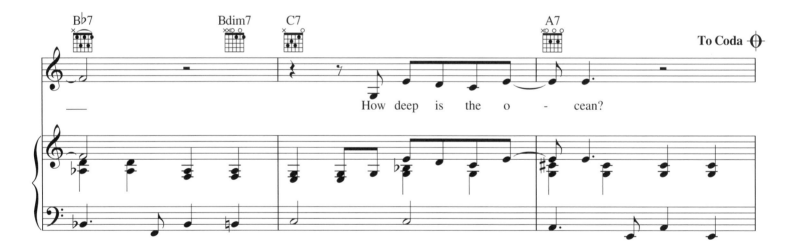

How deep is the o - cean?

To Coda ⊕

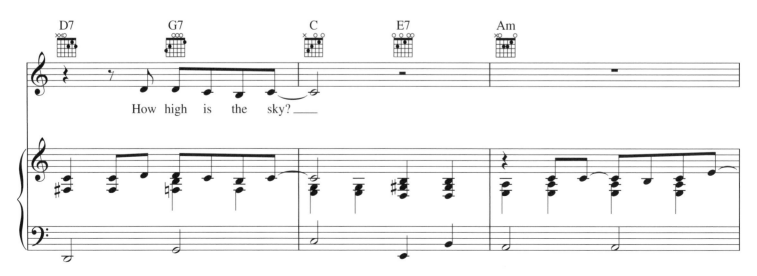

How high is the sky? _____

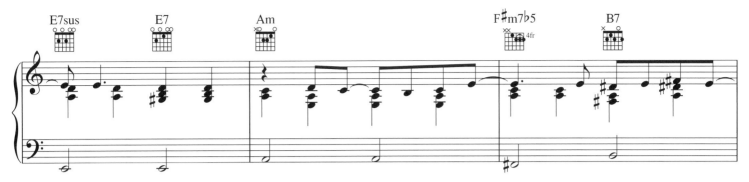

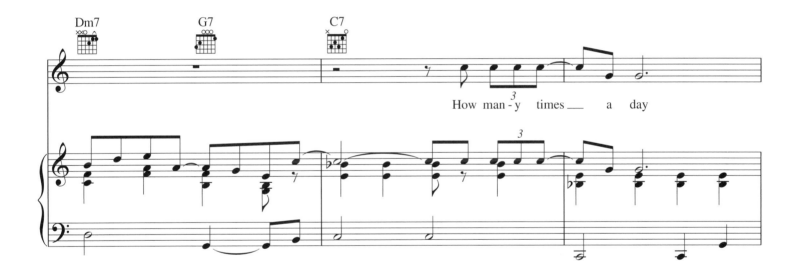

How man-y times ___ a day

do I think of you? ___

How man-y ros-

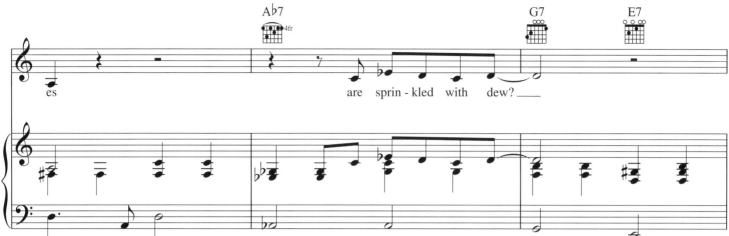

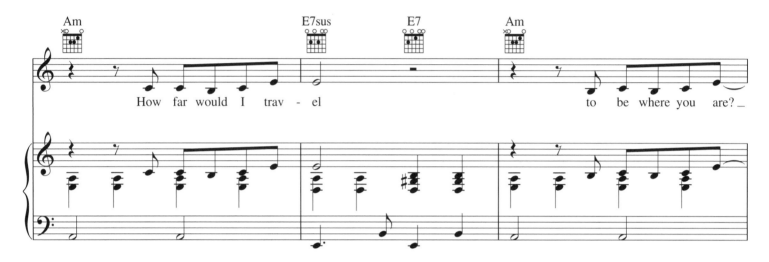

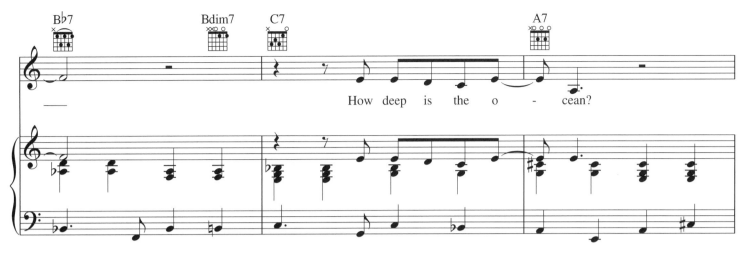

How deep is the o - cean?

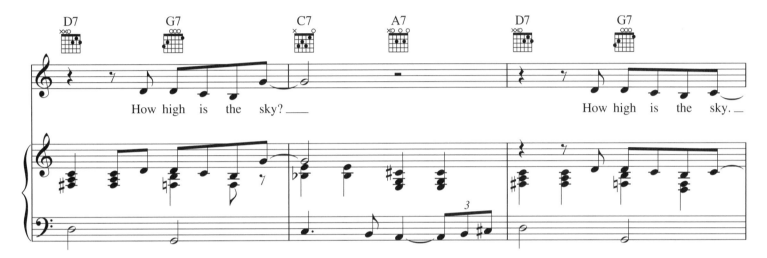

How high is the sky? ____ How high is the sky. __

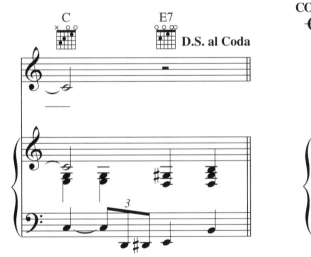

D.S. al Coda

CODA

How high is the sky? ___

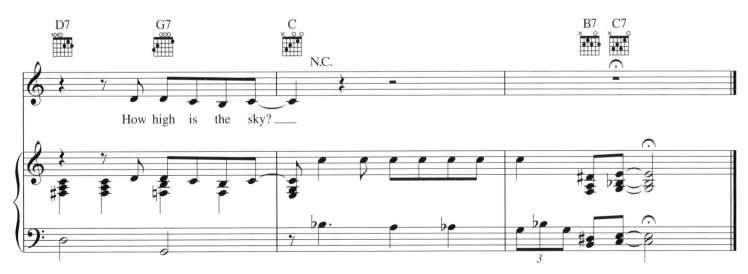

N.C.

How high is the sky? ____

MY VERY GOOD FRIEND, THE MILKMAN

Words by JOHNNY BURKE
Music by HAROLD SPINA

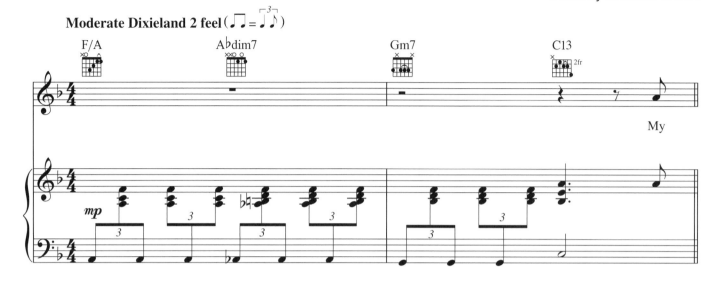

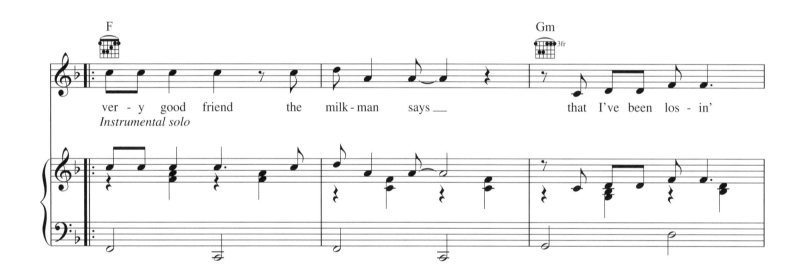

ver - y good friend the milk - man says __ that I've been los - in'
Instrumental solo

too much sleep. __ He does - n't like __ the hours I keep __ and

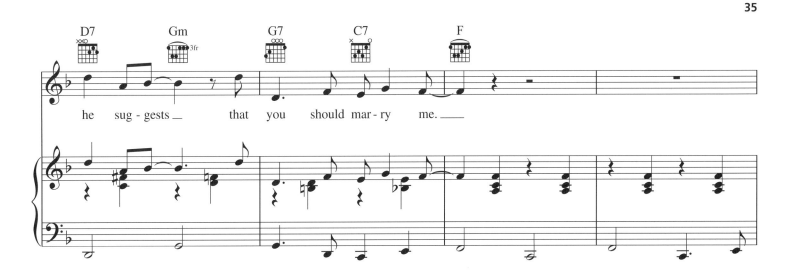

he sug - gests ___ that you should mar - ry me. ___

My ver - y good friend the

mail - man says ___ that it would make his bur - den less. ___

We both have the same ad - dress ___ and he sug - gests ___ that

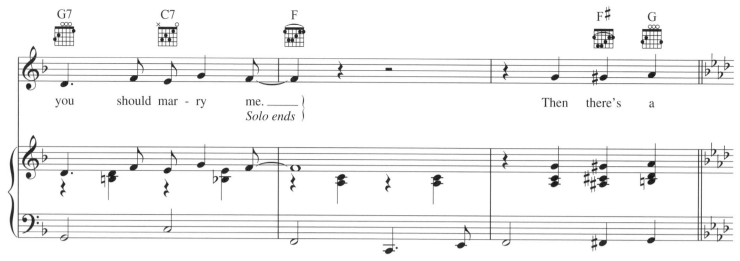

you should mar - ry me. _____ *Solo ends* Then there's a

ver - y friend - ly fel - low who prints all the lat - est real es - tate news. __

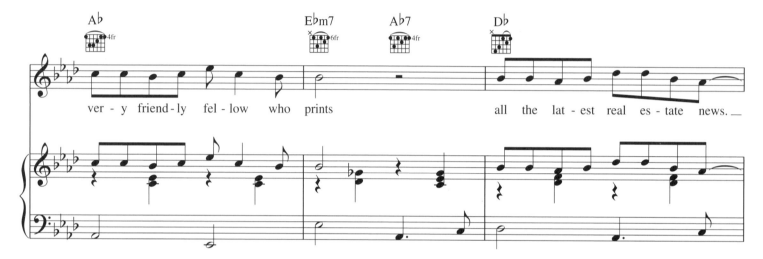

_____ And ev - 'ry day he sends me blue - prints of

cot - tag - es with __ coun - try views. My ver - y good friends the

neigh - bors say ___ they've been watch - in' lit - tle things ___ I do. ___

And they per - cieve that I love you, ___ so I sug - gest ___ that

you should mar - ry me. ___

Here comes the bride all fat and wide.

CAN'T HOLD OUT MUCH LONGER

Words and Music by
WALTER JACOBS

Slow Blues

won - der do you ev - er think of me? ____

You know I'm wild a - bout you, ba - by, but you ____

don't care noth - in' in the world for me. ____

Instrumental solo

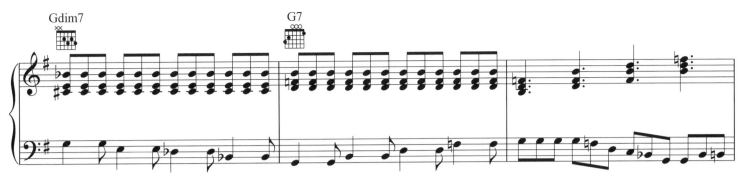

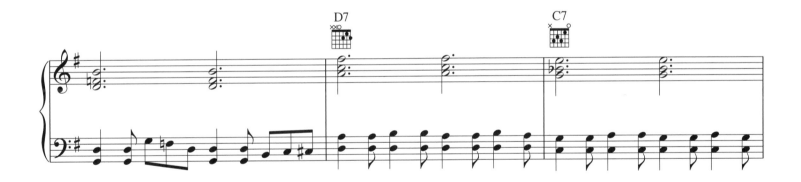

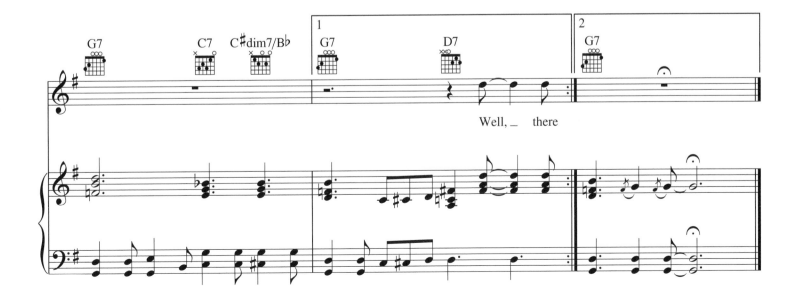

Well, __ there

THAT'S NO WAY TO GET ALONG

Words and Music by
REV. ROBERT WILKINS

Well, I'm

go - in' home. (Well, I'm go - in' home.) _ Friends, sit _ down, (Friends, sit _ down.) _ And
low _ down _ (these low _ down) Wom-en, ma - ma. _ (wom-en, ma-ma.) _ Well, they
treat-ed me _ (they treat-ed me) _ like my poor heart _ (like my poor heart) _ was

long.
long.
long.

'Cause these
They

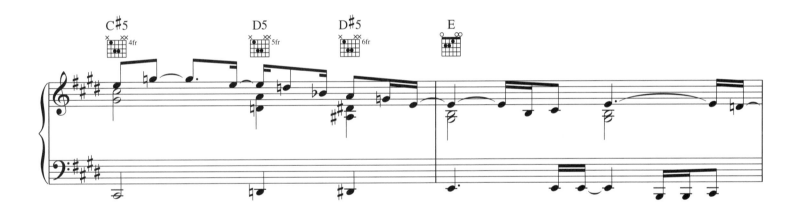

Well, I've   stood   on ___ (Well, I've   stood _ on) ___ the
want _ some _ (I   just   want _ some,) train   to   come _

that's no way for me ___ to get a - long.

I just

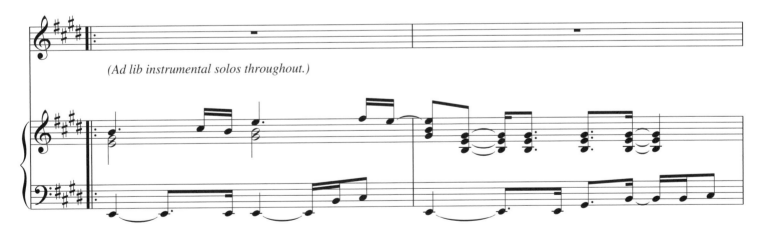

(Ad lib instrumental solos throughout.)

Optional Ending

Repeat and Fade

EVERYTHING WILL BE ALRIGHT

Words and Music by
J.J. CALE

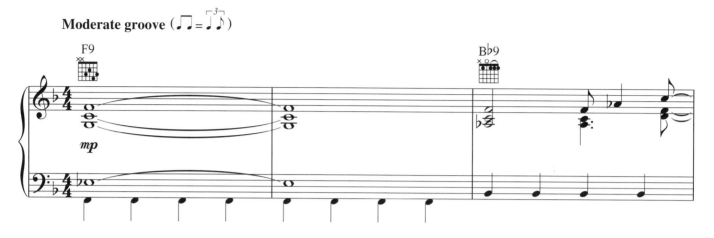

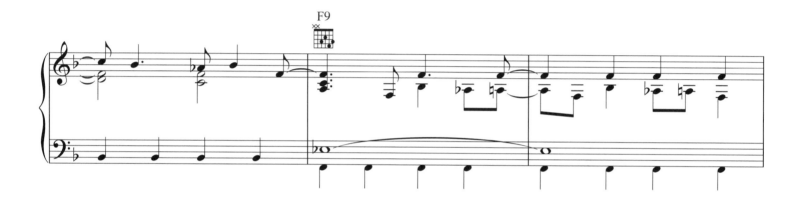

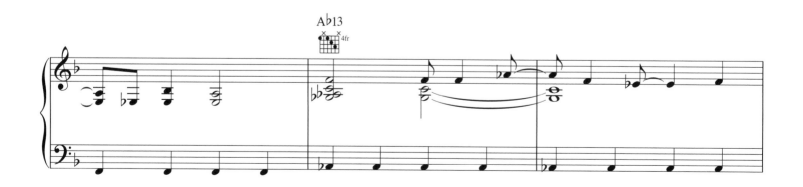

Same old has - sle ev - 'ry night, ____
You get your ____ gun, I'll ____ get mine. ____

all we do ____ is fuss ____ and fight. ____
We can do ____ it just ____ one time. ____

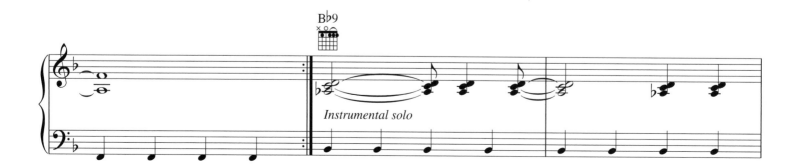

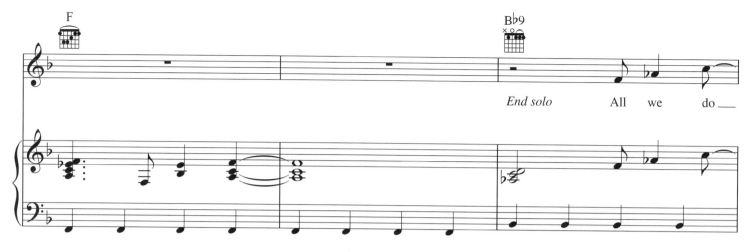

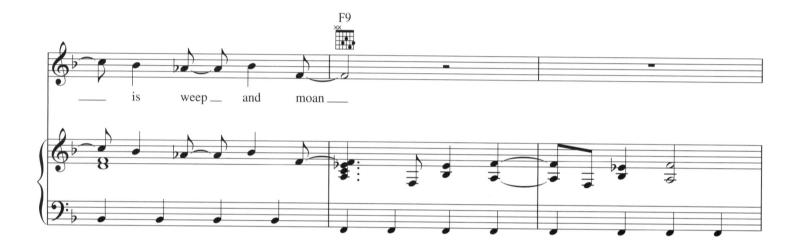

Ain't no use ____ de - ny - in' _____ ev - 'ry - thing ____

____ will be ____ al - right. ____

Instrumental solo

DIAMONDS MADE FROM RAIN

Written by DOYLE BRAMHALL II,
NIKKA COSTA and JUSTIN STANLEY

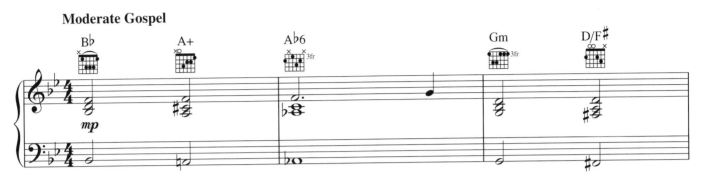

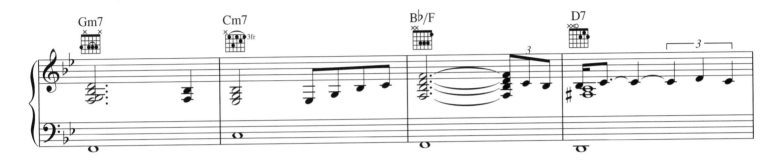

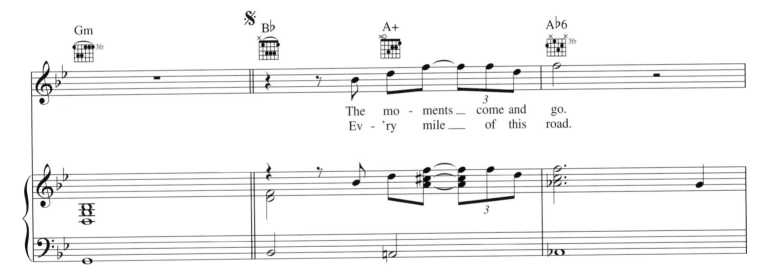

The mo - ments___ come and go.
Ev - 'ry mile___ of this road.

Ev -'ry mem -'ry___ leaves a trace.   All that I've
Ev -'ry chord that___ struck my soul.   You are the

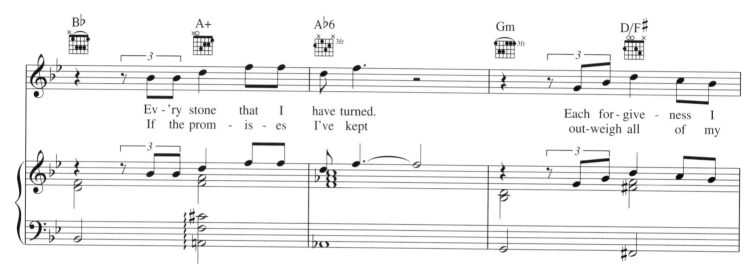

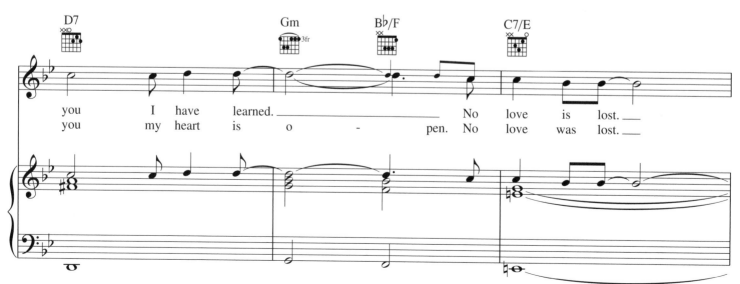

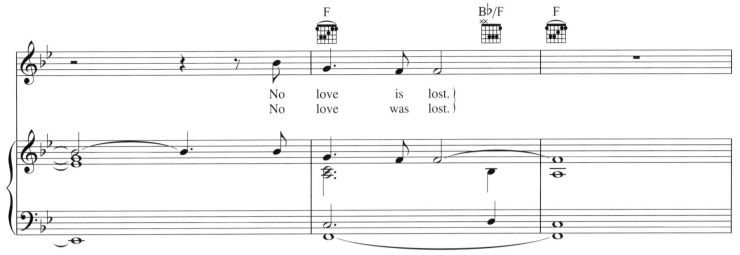

No love is lost.
No love was lost.

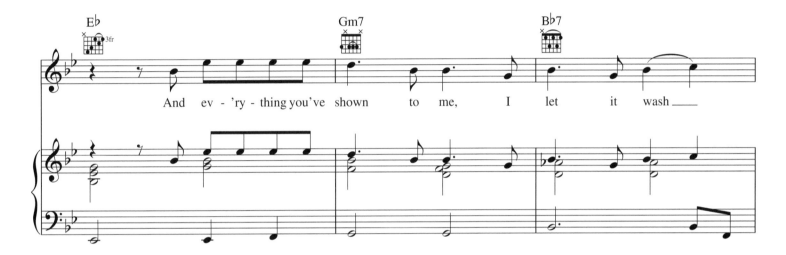

And ev-'ry-thing you've shown to me, I let it wash ___

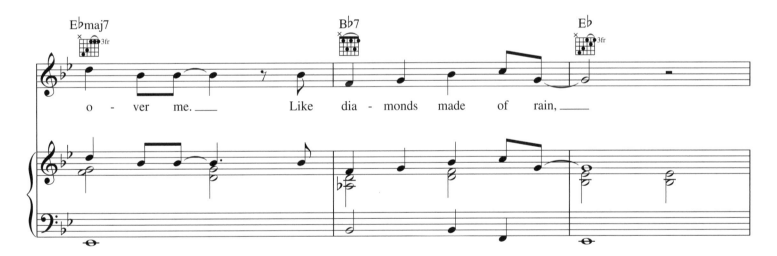

o - ver me. ___ Like dia-monds made of rain, ___

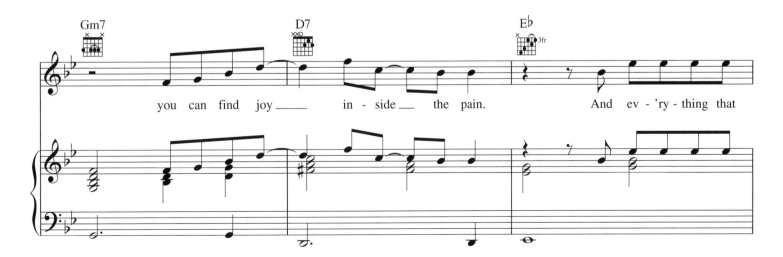

you can find joy ___ in - side ___ the pain. And ev-'ry-thing that

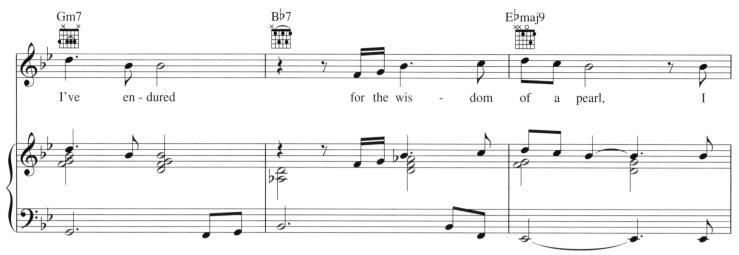

I've en-dured for the wis - dom of a pearl, I

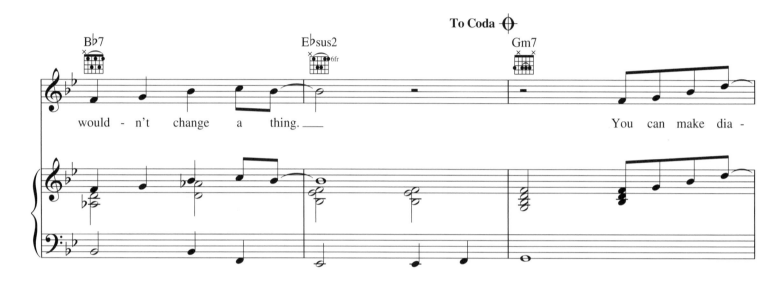

would - n't change a thing. ___ You can make dia -

To Coda

- monds from ___ the rain. ___

(Ad lib. instrumental solo.)

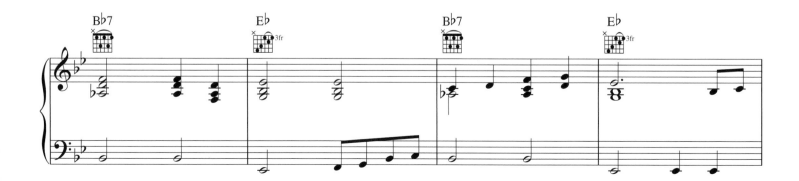

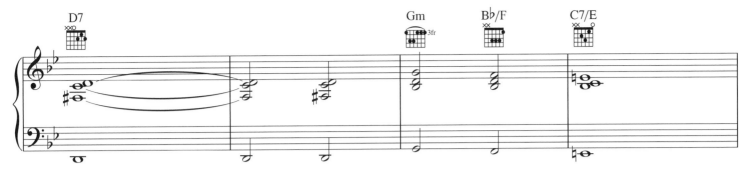

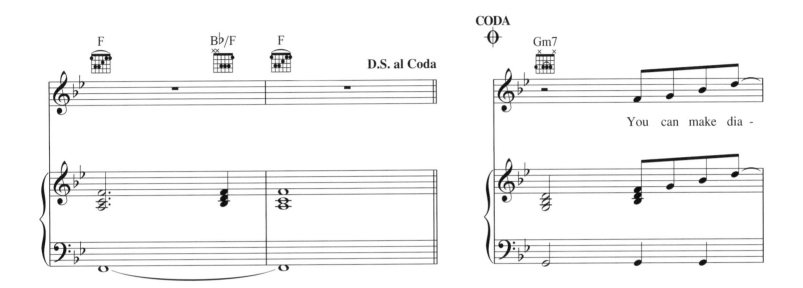

You can make dia -

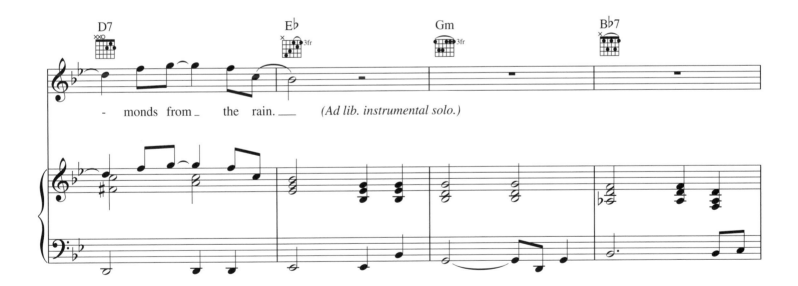

- monds from __ the rain. ___ *(Ad lib. instrumental solo.)*

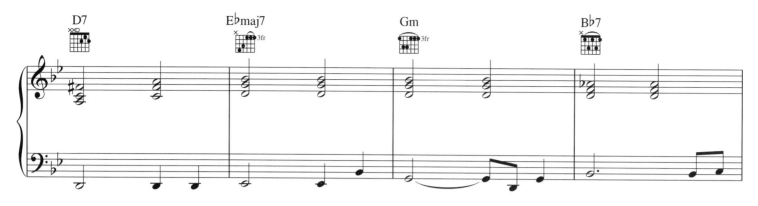

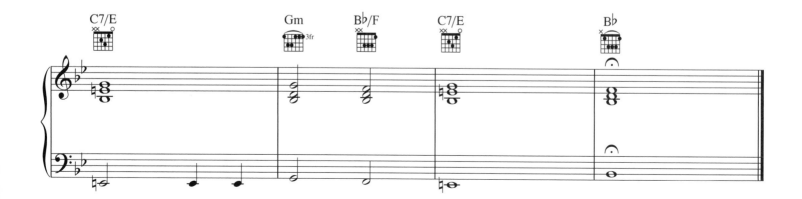

WHEN SOMEBODY THINKS YOU'RE WONDERFUL

Words and Music by
HARRY WOODS

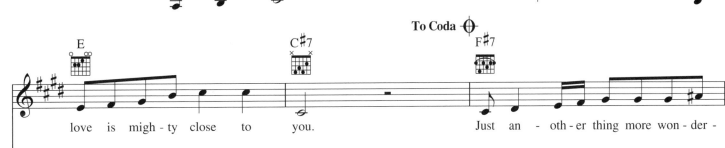

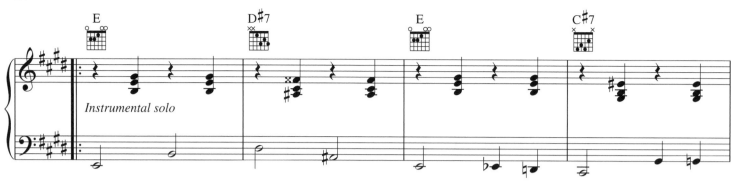

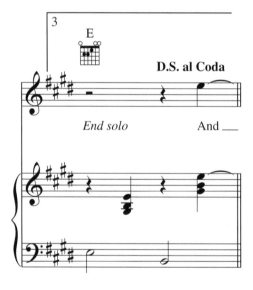

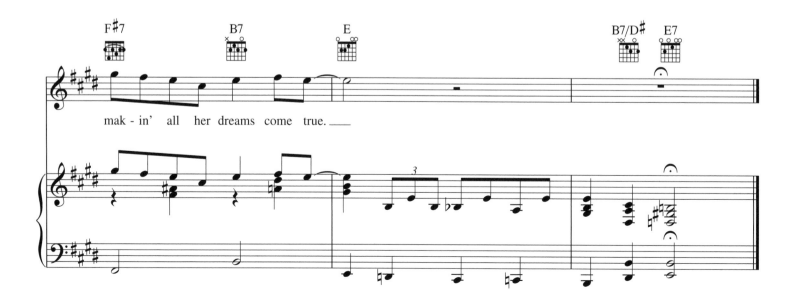

HARD TIMES BLUES

Words and Music by
LANE HARDIN

Moderate Blues

* *Recorded a half step lower.*

cry'n 'bout __ hard times,   they __ com-in' more and more. __
'bout these __ hard times,   they __ com-in' more and more. __
boss man __ told me   they ain't hir - in' an - y - more. __

Lord,   I
Well, ___

Well, _____ was a blue-bird, ba - by,

had my trunk packed on my back. _____

RUN BACK TO YOUR SIDE

Words and Music by ERIC CLAPTON
and DOYLE BRAMHALL II

Moderately fast Blues

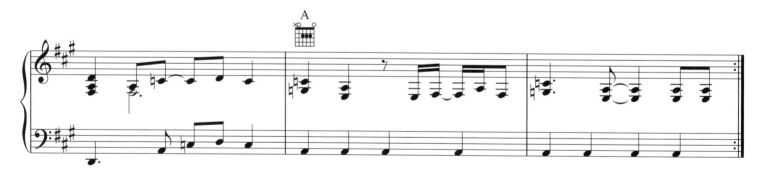

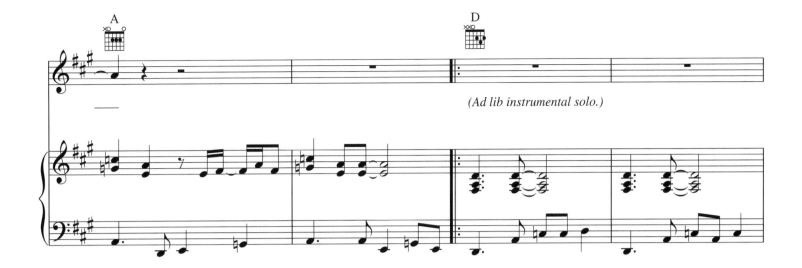

(Ad lib instrumental solo.)

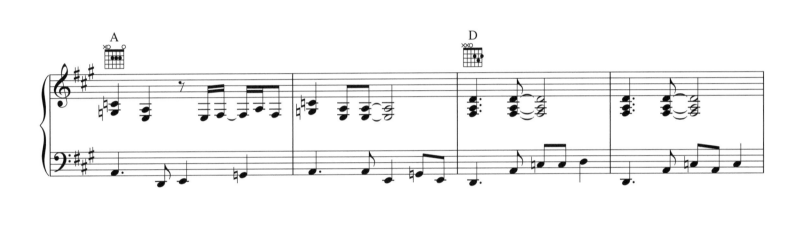

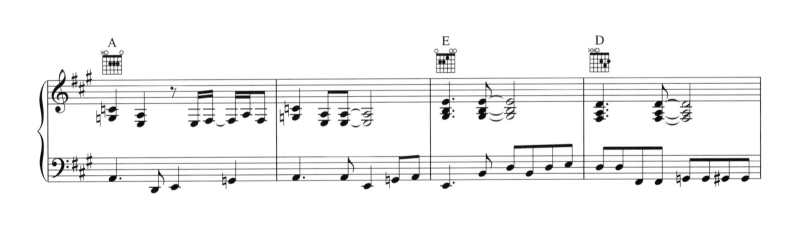

Well, _ I

don't wan - na be __ here when the sun __ goes down. __

I don't wan - na be __ here when the sun __ goes down. __

__ An - oth - er day go - in' no - where

in this lone - some town. __ I'm gon - na

run,
run back to your ___ side.

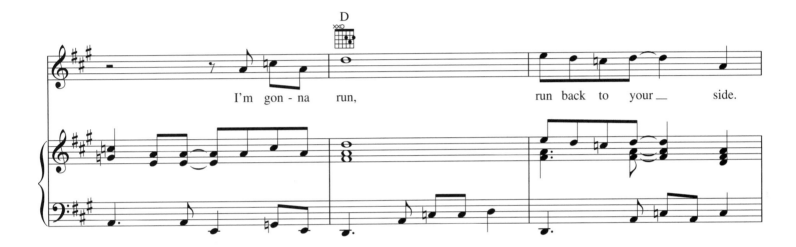

I'm gon-na run,
run back to your ___ side.

Well, ___ you know that I miss ___ you,

can't ___ be sat - is - fied. ___

1

I'm gon-na

(Ad lib instrumental solo.)

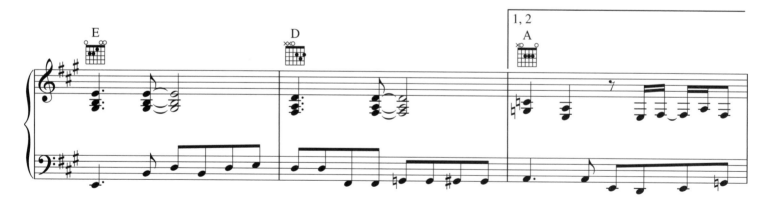

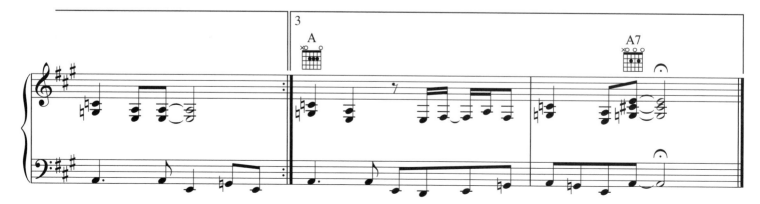

AUTUMN LEAVES

English lyric by JOHNNY MERCER
French lyric by JACQUES PREVERT
Music by JOSEPH KOSMA

The fall-ing leaves ____
Instrumental solo

drift by my win-dow, the au-tumn leaves ____

of red and gold. ____   I ____ see your lips, ____

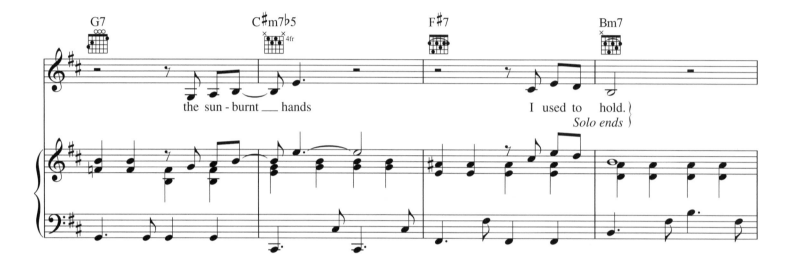

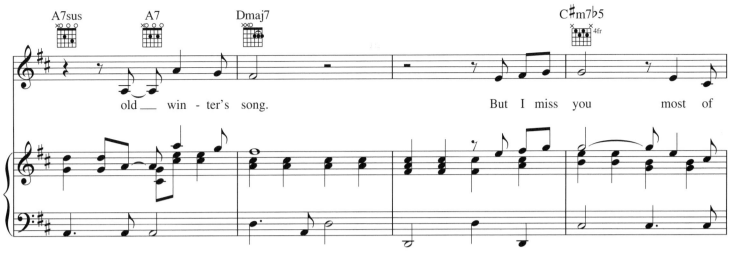

when au - tumn leaves ___ start to

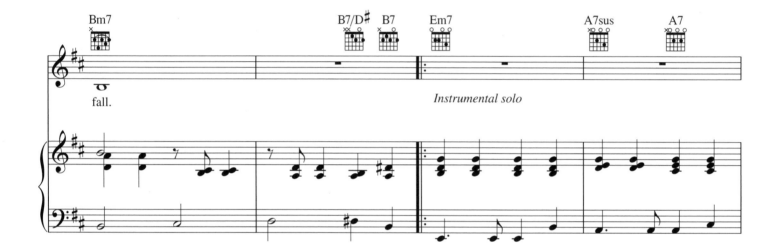

fall.

Instrumental solo

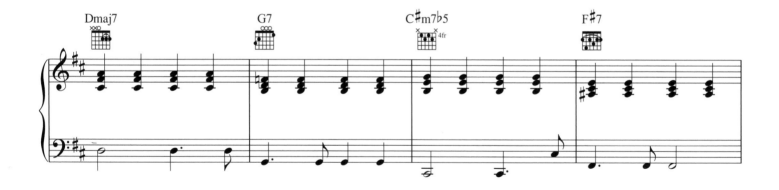

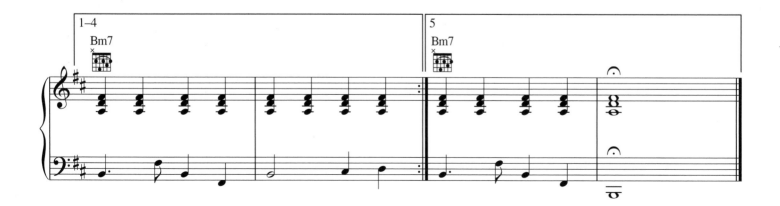